Shatters in Time

Emily DeBeck

Presentation by *BookLeaf Publishing*

Web: www.bookleafpub.com

E-mail: info@bookleafpub.com

ISBN: 9789395755160

First edition 2022

Annihilation

I told myself this would never happen again
yet I fell to it another time.
Wish fulfilment.
Yearning.
Naiveté of the highest degree.
Diagnose me
I am a pretty fool.
Only
I am not so pretty anymore.
I am an imposter.
This heart is a forfeiture
a petty offering of someone else's maybe.
All it takes
is a smile.
All it takes
is to look like you
and the opportunity to feel like someone else.
No wonder
it never lasts.
No wonder
I lost everything.
I am no longer pretty
but I am still a fool.
I search for facades
and hope that this will be the last one
to obliterate me.

Let this annihilation
prove everything.
That everything
was in fact
nothing
at all.

Tenderness

Your silence is a proclamation of tenderness.
An expression of the unspoken,
words suspended in anguish.

I love you too,
but maybe love
is not what I can give you.

I'm sorry.
I'm no good at this.

Destruction

If I relinquished the pain,
would you still be there?

Are you sensation,
or are you only memory?

Everything fades,
but if we fade with it
did it ever exist at all?

If we are nothing but blips in time
I want your blip to be in sync with mine.
That we might press forward
Unhindered
but tethered
into permanency.

Together
We could be one.

We call this attachment
but truly
it is mutually assured destruction.

Damnation

All that I have left to say
Are things that I will regret.
I must quench the unspoken
And revel in the times
Pain did not consume
this eternal fondness
turned damnation.
The bitter and infinite unraveling
of our casual destruction.

The Gulls

There are ways to destroy yourself utterly
and not know the consequences 'til
you're shucked out from the bone
and your marrow is feast to the gulls.
Ever hungry
Screeching for more, more, more.

Thunderstorm

Like a thunderstorm
You crashed into my life
The downpour almost drowned me.
But still the sun erupted
On the other side
Dispelled the darkness
Of the storm clouds in your wake.
I see your face in puddles
But I know
They too will disperse.
What power there is
In surviving a natural disaster
From the beginning
To the end.

No Matter

No matter
our catastrophe.
No matter
our estrangement.
Life presses on
never once asking,
during its capricious ascent,
Are you with me?
or
Where would you like to go?

Embrace

If I had known
It was the last time we would embrace each
other
I would have held you longer.
So tightly
That the imprint of your body would always be
on mine.
I would never forget
Your sturdiness
Keeping me strong
Long after you were gone.

Horizon

Nowhere
are we more confined than in our minds.
I want out
but show me the way.
Guide me with smiles and soft touches
lend me the strength of your encouragement.
Tell me the sun is out today
and I will forget my burdens, my shadows.
So together we can entwine our fingers
blazing forward
into a horizon of terrific possibilities.

Strawberries

If we could,
bind ourselves to infinity
I would think of strawberries and laughter.
Your eyes linked on mine
sharing an innocent world
pressed not for time,
only dumb luck.

Constant/Variable

If you were a constant,
I could be your variable.
I would accompany you through life's equations,
big and small,
and together we could find a solution,
imperfect,
but truly ours.

Dalliance

Let this early morning dalliance,
reach midday.
More time with you,
my darling,
is more time,
spent in the sun.

Illusion

Free me of this painstaking illusion.
All this time I thought I was running alongside
you
But these aching feet remind me
I was running after you.

Mercy

I want this mercy to be spoken aloud
I'm sorry if I have spent too long with my head
in the clouds.
See me, feel me
May our next moment be
Everything you could have ever imagined
And so much more.
Cry mercy
Mercy for you
And mercy for me.

Contemplation

Today's forecast:
Cloudy, with a chance of contemplation.
The times we shared,
and all the rest,
we never got to.

Absence

Sweet nothings
Are everything
In the hollow absence
You left me in.

Euphoria

I would like to take you into a place within my heart
Called Euphoria.
Beyond the blood and arteries
We could share our hopes and aspirations
Embrace moments
Cherish our achievements
And bolster each other in times of doubt.
Here,
I would welcome you with my life song.
Waiting to hear
Your gentle tune
Coalescing with mine.

Your Hand

I'd like to hold your hand a final time.
Trace the lines of past, present, and future.
I'd get to know you better this way.
Better than words could ever say.

Salvation

Speak in the mirror a thousand times
and marvel
how similar
you are
than to when you started.

(Could this reflection be our salvation?)

Forever

Forever I am the same
But to you
I feel different
Every time.

Ghost

I feel you
In the empty sheets of my bed
In the laughter of my chest.
I see you
In the places you once stood
In the spaces I have yet to clean.
I crave you
In all aspects of this new life without you.
Understand,
Part of me is still yours
and your memory
Is forever mine.
All this vacancy
Is still filled with your ghost.

www.ingramcontent.com/pod-product-compliance
Lightning Source LLC
Chambersburg PA
CBHW060928130726
48001CB00006B/2464